Learn

AN EASY PROCESS

Andrew Skidmore

Learning Ritual

AN EASY PROCESS

Andrew Skidmore

Lewis Masonic

First published 2012

ISBN 978 085318 399 0

Published by Lewis Masonic

an imprint of Ian Allan Publishing Ltd, Hersham, Surrey KT12 4RG.
Printed in England by Ian Allan Printing Ltd, Hersham, Surrey KT12 4RG.

Visit the Lewis Masonic website at www.lewismasonic.co.uk

Contents

Foreword
by
Graham Redman

The truly distinctive thing about Freemasonry is the way in which it teaches its lessons to its candidates and members. In this it differs significantly, for example, from clubs and societies where the benefits of membership are obtained by payment of a subscription, and from charities where the raising of money or the giving of time for a particular object is the unifying thread. Freemasonry uses its *ritual* as a means of teaching, and subsequently reinforcing, its principles and its tenets. It does this not only for the candidate, who is, or should be, the focus of every ceremony, but also for the other Brethren present, who are constantly reminded of the ceremonies they underwent and the instruction they received from them.

It follows from this that every Mason who undertakes a part in the ritual work should strive to render that work to the best of his ability. Relatively few Brethren are highly gifted ritualists, but far more than give themselves credit for it are capable of delivering a ceremony or part of a ceremony in a way that will impress the candidate in the right way – provided that they set about it properly.

Andrew Skidmore has produced in *Learning Ritual – An Easy Process* a highly readable short, but comprehensive, guide to understanding, learning and, above all, delivering Masonic ritual. It is written in a down-to-earth style and deals with many aspects, physical as well as psychological, of the process of learning.

Every young Brother about to step on to the first rung of the ladder of offices in a Lodge will benefit from reading the advice that the author gives, and from re-reading it many times as he progresses towards and through the Master's Chair.

Graham Redman
Past Grand Sword Bearer
Assistant Grand Secretary

January 2012

Introduction

One of the problems that most often plague Freemasonry is poor ritual. By this, I don't just mean not getting the words right, but that the ritual is drab and uninspiring, which subsequently fails to actually "teach" a candidate or recipient. Learning ritual by rote (parrot fashion, regurgitation), more often than not, will produce that kind of ritual!

Ritual can often be mediocre, but it doesn't have to be; anyone can do ritual well, provided they are completely honest with themselves and are prepared to follow a process and work hard. I won't shy away from the fact that you have to work hard to produce the kind of ritual that, deep down, you really want to do. "Nothing in – Nothing out."

There is an element of "theatrical" about well-delivered ritual and if you are honest with yourself and recognise your limitations, you will, by following a simple process, discover the actor within. Don't aim to be a Laurence Olivier or Noel Coward, albeit we probably all know someone who has the ability to deliver ritual in a very theatrical way, be yourself, but please recognise that delivery of any speech, talk or ritual does require the actor's confidence. We can all do it if we are shown how.

As a dear friend once said to me in his inimitably theatrical manner – and I quote . . . *"It's simply a case of teeth and tits dear boy . . . smile, stick your chest out and everyone will feel your confidence and competence."* Sadly, that friend of mine is no longer with us, but the value of his advice lives with me every day. Thank you, Brother Athol.

Very briefly, let me tell you a little about my mentor, W.Bro Athol Cameron McDonald. Athol was my proposer into Freemasonry and it was no great surprise to find that he was indeed a member of the Craft. Athol was a great actor, a most reliable and knowledgeable man and Mason, charitable and compassionate. He was also a real character too. When I first saw Athol performing ritual, some lengthy piece which I really believed only an actor's skills could produce, I was amazed. I distinctly remember saying to myself, *"I could never do that"*. The sad thing is that for a time, I truly believed that I would never aspire to be one of the "Athols" of this world. It took a while before I asked Athol and others how the devil they managed to do what they did so well and the answer that came back was simple: commitment, practice, hard work and more of the same. The actor would come if I was prepared to do as I was directed (to tell you the truth, I was told rather than directed, but then again that was Athol).

I will be totally honest with you that the thought of working hard when it wasn't career related was alien to me. I thought Freemasonry was a hobby and to be enjoyed, not to have to put yourself under the pressure of having to learn ritual and attend loads of rehearsals just to get it right! Doesn't a hobby come under the category of leisure?

Looking back I am almost ashamed of what I now see as a selfish and inconsiderate attitude. Of course the work had to be put in to get the results. I was involved in martial arts for a number of years, and quite successfully too. I trained every day and regularly put demands on my body of a most torturous physical nature. Why? Simply because I wanted to be the best I could be.

Strangely enough, I have never bled nor even broken into a sweat learning my ritual, but, my goodness, have I worked hard! Actually, it isn't hard; it's mostly a matter of knowing how to do it, plus the required commitment and a lot of practice.

This book is intended to impart some guidelines on how to do "Good Ritual". Initially it doesn't really require any particular talent, just drive and self-belief to do well. With practice you should be able to use these techniques to good effect in your masonic career. I use the word "career" because I truly believe that Freemasonry is a career, especially when taken seriously.

The difference I have noticed between my Masonic career and my former professional career is that when given a responsibility in Freemasonry, such as an office or a piece of work, your Masonic peers genuinely wish you well and will do all they can to help you succeed, whereas professional "so called well-wishers" are really saying . . . *"Well done on your promotion. (It should have been me.)"* Call me cynical, I don't mind.

Do you fear memorising your ritual?

Let me offer you a simple example of how the fear of memorising the words, to a degree, is a myth.

The Bedtime Story

Imagine this . . . you are asked to read a child a bedtime story . . . you sit on the edge of the bed or in the rocking chair close by. You ask the question, *"What story shall we read tonight?"* To your surprise the child hands you a book that you have never seen or heard of before; the author, the characters, in fact the whole thing feels almost alien to you. The little child says, "Read it to me, then" and you sit there almost lost. The lack of familiarity is surely going to make it harder to read it with conviction. After all, how can you possibly get into character if you don't know the character? The character names and place names are unusual and unfamiliar. It doesn't mean that you lack the intelligence to read the story; it simply means that you don't know the story. So the first time you read it, you do so as if you have just popped into the airport shop to read a novel on the flight home. You open the first page having no idea what lies ahead. The difference is that this time you aren't reading it to yourself, but you have an audience, a very important audience who will be so disappointed if you don't do a decent job. So you read on and the next night . . . you guessed it, the same storybook is dropped into your hand accompanied by a look of expectation that maybe this time it will be a little more exciting. You read on. This happens for several nights and almost unknown to you, you get into character. You find your tongue is easily rolling the previously awkward characters' and place names. The emphasis and intonation are enhancing the story and bringing it from the page into the room. After several days, you find that you are looking less at the pages and more at the reaction of your audience. The need to look at the words or maybe a picture is simply to prompt you as to what part of the story comes next.

Imagine the horror when the child wants the same story one night and you can't find the book. You search high and low, but no joy. What to do? *"Go on then"* says the child, *"you know the story, tell it to me."* So you sit there with the look of all the characters in the book ready to burst from your face . . . and you start telling the story. Probably with the best and most surprising result you could imagine. You know your way around the story and are fully aware of the places and characters, to the extent that you have a vivid picture of every part etched in your mind's eye, only to appear as and when the story calls for them.

Ask yourself one question . . . when did you set out to memorise the words? Ritual is not too different. In most cases it's a story, involving places, characters, dates and times and many happenings, just like the child's story that we have just become a very, very important part of.

Chapter 1

Getting Ready to Learn

There are a number of different things that you may want to do to assist you in getting ready to learn; in other words, to get your head right and avoid distraction. However, one of the things that you will always have to do is to make sure that you are in the learning mode. This is very important because you have to be ready to take on board all that you are attempting to learn. You have to be ready to pay attention, and it can be very difficult to pay attention if the subject is complicated and/or you just aren't ready to do your best. This means that, for you to take it all in, you have to know how to make sure you are ready to learn and pay attention.

There are typically three basic things that you will have to do before you start learning. First, try to make sure that you are not over-tired. This is important because the more tired you are, the more difficult it will be for you to focus on the material that you are covering. In fact, not getting enough sleep may not only make it more difficult for you to focus on the information but it may also make it more difficult for you to understand the information that you are attempting to learn. This is because it's very easy to miss some of the key details of a complicated concept when you're already falling asleep. How many times have you been reading a book in bed, just before you drop off to sleep, and had to re-read the chapter the very next night? This is not to say that reading just prior to falling asleep is a bad thing. On the contrary, often facts and statistics will stick in your memory and the recall of those facts etc is often easier. Personally I find that facts stick but stories do not.

Secondly, try to make sure that you eat before you start. Again, this is important because hungry people, just like tired people, have more trouble focusing on material than individuals that are well fed. This means that you have to have some sort of meal before you start. This is simply to ensure that you're thinking about ritual and not your stomach.

Thirdly, when you're not feeling 100%, or are under the weather, consider putting off learning until you feel up to it. This is important because you will typically have more trouble focusing on the information that you need to take on board when you're sick. This means that you will typically be better off if you avoid trying to study and get some sleep. It's a well-known fact that you will be able to recover from your illness sooner and get back into the learning mode more quickly. This of course refers to the normal cold or flu-like illnesses and not the more serious conditions. Obviously if the meeting is within the very near future, and a rehearsal is planned, try your best to attend, even if it is simply for the benefit of others taking part.

Now I know what you are thinking, *"Why is he stating the obvious?"*, but many times we try to do things under duress, rather than make the sensible decision to hold back until we are physically and mentally ready.

Maslow's Hierarchy

Maslow's hierarchy is a brilliant piece of study that in many ways is complicated, yet does explain how the science of behaviour and mental processing is an intrinsic part of producing a top performance.

Maslow's hierarchy

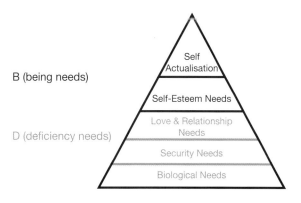

I'll give you the gist of what Maslow's hierarchy states and you can delve deeper if you need to qualify exactly what he's saying.

In brief, the message is stating, in a somewhat thorough and complicated way, that you have to be comfortable with yourself, accept your surroundings and feel that you couldn't be more ready to learn if you tried. The detail he goes into is important but so long as you feel motivated and have done all you can to get ready to learn, the actual act and process of learning become less of a chore.

If you have time to investigate Maslow's hierarchy in more detail it may be helpful to highlight the elements that you feel either have detrimentally impacted on past performances or perhaps will impact on a future performance. Don't be shy and be totally honest with yourself.

Chapter 2

Learning Styles

*"The man who never makes a mistake has
never done anything."*

As you are no doubt aware, we all learn in different ways. For many of us, the first obstacle is identifying our preferred order of learning styles. I say "styles" because we do use all styles – Visual, Verbal, Tactile, Aural, and Kinaesthetic, albeit in varying degrees of preference. I can't stress enough how important it is to identify your main learning style, or combination of learning styles. If we take a good look at all styles, that should help you identify one or more styles and therefore take the first important step in "Learning Ritual".

Visuals literally see what they are saying from the actual page of the ritual book from which they have been studying. If this is your preferred style and you have performed ritual previously, then you will probably recall a time when you have been going through a piece with someone who is checking your accuracy and can tell that person when to turn the page. Also, your ritual book or script will be full of notes and directions, even drawings of perambulation if you hold a floor office, such as a Craft Deacon, or Royal Arch Sojourner, or if you will be interacting with such an officer. You may highlight keywords or phrases that prompt you to move on or physically move to a particular place. Visuals don't need to be told why they do things in a particular order, they see the reason why. Visuals would enjoy delivering a lecture using props, such as a Tracing Board, or Working Tools rather than reciting a large piece of text, such as the charge after initiation.

Verbals have to hear and/or see the actual language. They make copious notes, even though they already have the words, and that way they transfer what they are given into their language. They very often re-write their notes. If you look at the notes they make they will have additional notes/comments in the margin. If you explain something to a Verbal, they often paraphrase things back to you, again transferring what you have said into their language rather than showing that they understand – that way truly understanding. Most people are Verbals or have a degree of Verbal to accompany their preferred learning style. Unlike Visualism, Verbalism is a learning style and not a presentation style.

Tactiles need to hold things. The actual touch of an item of relevance immediately creates a bond or relationship. Hence when a Tactile refers to an object, for example a Masonic Working Tool, he can physically feel it in his hand and as a result see it in his mind's eye, even though he may not be holding it at that moment. A Tactile, given the opportunity, will learn early and can demonstrate an intuitive approach as to how things work. If a Tactile is given the opportunity to take something apart and rebuild it, the knowledge of that item gained is quite incredible. I am not suggesting for one moment that if you find yourself to be a Tactile that you dismantle the lodge furnishing, but you may well be the best person when such a task is required.

Aurals are those who we refer to as having "fantastic memories". These people seem to have an encyclopaedic knowledge of all things they become involved in; they can do a piece of work that they haven't done for years and only need a quick refresh to perform it well. You find that Aurals study very hard, but once they learn something, they have it for ever. Aurals often find it hard to understand that we are not all that way inclined and sometimes assume that others are either not as bright or as committed as they are.

Kinaesthetic learning is a style in which learning takes place by using the body in order to express a thought, an idea or an understanding of a particular concept (which could be related to any field). Some would say that Kinaesthetic and Tactile learning processes are the same, because they both demonstrate a high level of physical activity. Study, however, would indicate that a person with a Kinaesthetic bent appears more animated. That is because the use of their body is required to comprehend and subsequently demonstrate. For example, if one were explaining a term of measurement, such as a cubit (the first recorded unit of length, commonly referred to in certain Masonic rituals), rather than simply saying, *"A cubit is the distance between the fingertips and the elbow which on an average person measures about 24 digits or 6 palms or 1½ feet; this is about 45 cm or 18 inches,"* they would move around actually using their body to demonstrate. Quite simply, the more they use their body with movement to understand a concept, the easier they can recall it later. A really good example of one who learns via this style would be a dancer. Obviously they need to be aware of exactly what is required of their body at a given time and place.

To sum up this complicated and difficult to understand learning style, Kinaesthetics need to manipulate things. These are the people who physically need to take an object and put it with another object to know that there are now two objects. Kinaesthetics prefer not to work with theory as much as they like to take physical objects and change them. People who are identified as Kinaesthetics are often also Tactiles.

If you have already identified your Learning Style/s then you are ready to move forward.

To sum up, research shows that the above learning styles are split into two main categories: Passive Learning and Active Learning.

With Passive Learning, people generally remember 10% of what they read, 20% of what they hear, 30% of what they see and 50% of what they see and hear.

With Active Learning, people remember 70% of what they say and write and 90% of what they say and do.

The 10% is obviously taking the paper or book and reading it. If you take your ritual and simply read it through a few times then you are likely to remember about 10%, but don't see that as a negative and discard what is a most important part of the process. Let's face it, if you do this often enough in the early stages then you relieve the pressure from other, maybe less preferred, learning styles.

The 20% of what you hear can simply be listening to yourself either saying it live, (which also incorporates the 10% of reading), or maybe recording it on to some form of recording device (I even use my mobile phone to record short pieces) and then playing back as often as you can. Your own voice is far more palatable than someone else's voice, especially when we try to "over speak" the recording. It almost feels rude to interrupt someone else's voice, don't you feel?

As for the 30% of what you see, you do have to get your mindset right. If you are watching someone else perform a piece of ritual, or a particular office, then make sure that you pay attention. This is really important with regard to the many progressive offices which Freemasonry places you in. For example, as an Inner Guard in a Craft Lodge, you should be studying the Junior Deacon, not only what he has to say in the various ceremonies but the perambulations for a particular ceremony and where he has to be when he speaks. That way you have cleverly and often unwittingly linked these two different learning styles together; you listen and watch, so you hear 20% and see 30%! That's the 50% of what you see and hear.

Oh yes, the more that you do this the more these percentages will increase. It's all about focus. Don't let anyone distract you. Don't be afraid to tell someone who may be sat near to you, *"Sorry, but I'm trying to concentrate on the Junior Deacon. I'm doing it next year and I need to hear what he's saying and see what he's doing."*

If there is one message with regard to the progressive offices, then I suppose this is it. Don't wait until next year, when you are in the office, before you try to learn the ritual and perambulations of that office . . . do it now!

In my mother lodge we make all of the officers aware that the offices are not naturally progressive. If they don't perform their current office adequately and demonstrate their commitment, they do not automatically move up the ladder.

I have a slight issue with people jumping in and saying, *"I prefer to learn actively."* I feel that is so often a bit of a get-out. Of course active learning is important but without applying yourself to the necessary and often hard work of what I refer to as the preparation style, then leaping right in and getting active is where the poor quality ritual is demonstrated. Yes, I can hear people saying how much easier it is to get hands on and actually do the ritual, and I don't disagree, but if you apply yourself to the less

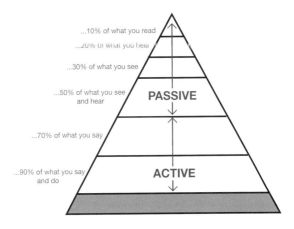

Research shows that we tend to remember what we learn...

...10% of what you read
...20% of what you hear
...30% of what you see
...50% of what you see and hear

PASSIVE

...70% of what you say
...90% of what you say and do

ACTIVE

stressful task of listening and watching then when you start doing, the results are often much more rewarding. For those who insist that active learning is their preferred learning style then the lodge or class of instruction is a must.

Chapter 3

Lodge of Instruction

A very important part of getting ready to learn is being aware that, through your Lodge of Instruction, you can obtain an enormous amount of help and information. I can't stress enough the importance of joining your local Lodge (or Class) of Instruction. Every good ritualist will tell you that their time attending a Lodge of Instruction was time well spent. When I say "good ritualist" I don't necessarily mean someone who is word perfect, I mean a Freemason who can demonstrate that he has worked hard to deliver the ritual to the very best of his ability.

For those who don't know how a Lodge of Instruction is structured, it is usually managed by a Preceptor and in many cases supported by Assistant Preceptors. Such lodges operate within a geographical area or from a local Masonic building and provide training in the performance and understanding of the Craft and the ritual. The Preceptor is an elected position and is usually a Freemason who has spent several years as a Director of Ceremonies in his local lodge and is considered an authority in both the ritual and the Freemasonry in general. Whilst membership of a Lodge of Instruction is available to all Master Masons, many Preceptors allow Entered Apprentices and Fellow Craft to attend as a sort of associate member; that is to say that they do not have to pay any subscriptions and do not have voting rights, but can get involved in all ceremonial up to and including their respective degree.

So what can you expect when attending a Lodge of Instruction? Well generally the dress code is casual but smart. The lodge will normally open much later than a regular lodge and you may well be asked to take an office up to and even including that of Worshipful Master. The agenda is in many ways similar to your regular lodge, but generally less detailed; that is to say that the risings rarely have correspondence for Grand Lodge or Provincial, District or Metropolitan Grand Lodge. You will find that they almost always include an item which will provoke some form of forum or discussion. This is where you are given the opportunity to ask questions of the Preceptors.

Hopefully your Lodge of Instruction will be so popular that you will have to put your name down in advance to practise a specific office, which may well be an office you plan to hold in your regular lodge at some time in the near future. What an opportunity!

The sad thing is that so often Lodges of Instruction are used as a rehearsal for the forthcoming ceremony. I hear this many times when at a regular lodge meeting a brother gives a report that "*At the last Lodge of Instruction, we practised the ceremony of Initiation, or Passing or Raising,*" and that is the ceremony they have just performed. As a Preceptor myself, I cannot too strongly recommend Lodge of Instruction. It's a golden opportunity to get a taste of things to come, in an environment which is far more relaxed than a regular lodge meeting. Oh yes . . . it's also a great opportunity to socialise with the other brethren too!

Chapter 4

Understanding the Ritual

Figure out the Words

Once you have identified your preferred learning style(s), the first step to learning any ritual is to know what you're saying! This should be obvious, but is often overlooked because we are often reluctant to admit that we don't already know the right words. Don't be afraid to recognise your own limits – I've never met anyone yet who gets every single word right every time.

If you take the ritual and the very first thing you do is read it through, you can bet that there will almost always be words that you either have never used before or that you are not sure of their meaning. The meaning of a word can vary, dependent on the context in which it is being used. An example which will highlight this is the answer to that age-old question . . . What is Freemasonry? The answer, as we all know, is *"A peculiar system of morality, veiled in allegory and illustrated by symbols."* When we read the word peculiar, we see an adjective that is often used to describe something in a somewhat derogatory manner – something or indeed someone who is "queer, odd or strange" or something that has happened that could be described as "out of the ordinary". It could be a reference to someone's habit, such as the taking of snuff, or the hobby of collecting some particular species of insect. The intended meaning, in this context, is "something distinctive in nature" or "special in character".

If you adopt the following piece of advice before learning any piece, you will see a marked improvement in your understanding of the ritual:

- Read through once.
- Write down the words that you don't fully comprehend. (Be honest with yourself – you may be surprised how many words you list.)
- Note the words where you are unsure of the correct pronunciation
- Research the words, either on the internet or using a dictionary.
- Write down the meanings against each word on your list.
- Read through again and be amazed at the difference.

It's also always a good idea to listen to someone say the words, preferably several times. If the piece of the ritual is part of a progressive office, such as Junior Warden etc, you should be doing this the entire previous year, listening to your predecessor!

Listen carefully, and make sure you understand what's being said. Ask questions if you don't. (After the meeting of course.)

This is the point: to catch any mistakes you may be making, so read through the book or the part of the book that you are working on. This is a good time to sit down with someone who is familiar with the ritual, someone who has maybe performed it to an impressive level. Don't be afraid to ask them; they will probably be flattered by this and willing to help. I have always found that if you need help you should never be afraid to ask for it. Literally walk up to the person and say, *"Could you help me, please . . "* How can they say no to that?

Ask your chosen ritualist, wordsmith, or reliable Past Master, and talk through it, reading out of the book slowly. Have him correct any mistakes, and fill in the words you don't know. Take notes, because you will forget the corrections as soon as you're on your own.

Chapter 5

Understanding the Speech

This step gets overlooked even more often than the previous one. Read through the ritual a couple of times, and make sure you really grasp it. Don't just know the words – know what it's talking about. Find out who the characters being talked about are. Again, ask questions.

Now, start trying to understand the speech structurally. Any ritual is made up of components – separate pieces that are linked together. For example, a section may be talking about symbols, with three paragraphs per symbol: concrete meaning, abstract meaning, and purpose. Figure out what these pieces are – you'll use them later. Let me explain: "concrete meaning" refers to words that stimulate some kind of sensory response within. Used and understood properly, as you read the words, you can use your imagination in conjunction with your senses to experience what the words represent. In this context, concrete words can include, for example, wine, chisel, gavel, temple, pencil, poignard, sepulchre, etc.

Now try to picture, in your mind's eye, a glass of wine. Because this word is a concrete word, you are easily able to form a mental picture of it and because concrete diction appeals to the senses, it tends to involve you, the reader, far more than abstract diction does. If you say that the wine was "nice" or "good", you would be describing it in an abstract way, but to say that the wine is "sweet" or "dry", then you are describing it in a concrete way. Ask yourself now . . . can you taste that sweet wine, or can you see the wine because someone has described it as nice?

Concrete diction uses language in such a way that describes qualities so that they can be perceived with the five senses (sight, touch, taste, smell and hearing). Where concrete words immediately have an impact on the senses, abstract words or terms refer to ideas or concepts. They have no physical reference.

The purpose is the desired or intended effect or result. Let's say that you are delivering the working tools of an Entered Apprentice to a candidate. The result you should strive for is to do so in a clear and concise manner, thus ensuring that the message is not only delivered but also received. Another purpose could be the example of perambulation and how important it is to have the purpose firmly fixed when responsible for the candidate's journey . . . I say journey because I mean just that. Whenever we are charged with taking a candidate around as part of his particular ceremony, the whole purpose of the perambulation is to travel somewhere. It may be from one place to another, but there is always a purpose. If you understand why the perambulation or journey is necessary to get the ceremony across, then that journey makes more sense to you and a lot more sense to the candidate. I know it sounds corny, but you would never just jump in a car, with the aim of trying to reach a destination, without at least having an idea of where you are going or how you intend to get there.

An easy way to get a grip on the whole picture is to at least be aware of other participants' roles in the ceremony. So, for example, if you are interacting with a main player, such as the Worshipful Master, and when reading through the ritual you only read your part, then when the Worshipful Master addresses you, you will more than likely be totally surprised. What should be your cue can often be the thing that completely throws you, simply because you didn't read it in context. You don't have to learn the words of the other players, just be aware of their part in the story. It's amazing how many people will type out or write out their lines only and try to memorise them immediately. That is learning by rote and rarely produces convincing ritual.

Rote learning has a part to play in any learning process. A good example would be when learning the alphabet or multiplication tables, or simply trying to remember a telephone number. As silly as it may seem, taking the multiplication tables as an example, most children can often learn what a multiplication answer will be before they can actually calculate it.

Rote learning is sometimes criticised and referred to with such derogatory terms as regurgitation or parrot fashion, because one who engages in rote learning may give the impression of having wrongly understood what they have written or said! May I be so bold as to suggest that although learning an alphabet or remembering a telephone number is the ideal place to apply the learning by rote method, any ritual or script that is intended to be delivered in a meaningful way should be understood?

I have seen a ceremony performed in this way, which was virtually word perfect. The Worshipful Master delivered a complete ceremony, almost without missing a beat. BUT to say that it was monotone and lacked feeling and intonation was an understatement! You could see the candidate almost falling asleep it was so boring, yet what a feat of memory. The deliverer of this piece had worked so hard to remember the words that he forgot to understand them.

If one thinks of the ritual or a speech in terms of movements, places, rooms etc, it will definitely help. This is especially useful for longer pieces. Visualise the speech. To simply remember the words and try to get them in the correct order is harder than remembering them as part of a journey. Let me give you an example of what I mean . . .

Now try to remember (by rote) the following words:

Newspaper – Car Keys – Post – Briefcase – Dog – Kettle – Mobile Phone – Loose Change – Suit – Slippers.

To simply and quickly remember these words does take either a good memory or repeating them over and over again very quickly and then delivering them before you forget them. However, try adding a dimension of physical being to each of them and you will, a) quickly learn them, and more importantly, b) find it hard to forget them.

OK, here we go.

When I arrive home, I walk through my front door and pick the newspaper up from the hall floor. I then place my car keys on the table in the corner of the hall. I collect my post from the same table and leave my briefcase at the side of the hall table. I walk into the kitchen and make sure that my dog Clyde has food and water. I quickly fill the kettle and switch it on. There is a shallow glass bowl in the kitchen where I deposit my mobile phone and my loose change. While the kettle is boiling, I walk upstairs to my bedroom and remove my suit, slip into something relaxing and pop my slippers on. I then go back to the kitchen, make my coffee, sit down and chill.

Now if you follow the story, focusing on the perambulation and the words, you have a far better chance of remembering them. Try listing 10 words of your own choosing and then visualise using them in a familiar setting, maybe your own home, office or lodge room. Closing your eyes in the first instance may help.

Another example of this, which you may be more familiar with, is the canonical explanation of the Second Degree Lecture, which is a walk-through of King Solomon's Temple. This is why we use symbols in the first place because they are easy to learn and internalise. The meaning of "canonical", in this context, is where the words are reduced to the simplest and most significant form possible without loss of generality, eg a basic story line. When learning your ritual, before you work on it, read it over and over again and let it work on you.

Small Scale Learning

This is never anyone's favourite part; anyone can do it, but no one finds it simple. It's considerably easier if you do it right, though.

Having taken the necessary steps to find out what the

words mean, particularly in the context of the ritual, start out by reading the speech over and over. Don't move on to the next step until you can read it from the ritual book quickly, without breaks or hesitation. Read it out loud whenever you get the chance. This step is particularly important and skipped more often than any other. Don't skip it – this is how you get your brain and mouth trained to the words. It may sound silly, but it really matters. The mental pathways used to talk are distinct from those used to read.

Now, start trying to learn sentences – just sentences. Read the first word or two of the sentence, and then try to fill in the remainder from memory. Don't be too concerned if you can't do it immediately; it will probably take at least five or ten times before you're getting most of the sentences. You'll find some that are hard – hammer those ones over and over, but don't totally neglect the rest while you do so. Again, get to the point where you're doing reasonably well on this, before going on to the next step.

A trick I personally use is to hold the book or paper out in front of me so that I can see it easily and glance at the script if I feel that I really do need a prompt. Try and focus your eyes on something just above the page, such as a focal point on a wall, then when you absolutely need to, glance back at the page just to gain that prompt. The more you do this, the less you have to.

Larger Scale Learning

Once you've got most of the sentences, try to move on to paragraphs. Again, some will be easy and some hard. Try to understand exactly why this sentence follows that one. In most cases the ritual does make sense. An individual paragraph is almost always trying to express a single coherent thought, in pieces. Figure out what that thought is, and why all the pieces are necessary. Keep at this until you're able to get most paragraphs by glancing at the first word or two, or by thinking, *"Okay, this is the description of a twenty four inch gauge,"* or something like that. I would actually say that at this point in the process, you would probably be substituting certain words for the actual words on the page. Don't be concerned about that at this stage. If you are then it means that you are grasping the meaning of the ritual but can't quite be as accurate as you would like, or need to be. That's a massive positive sign. Accuracy will come as you progress and we will cover that later.

Finally, start putting it all together. This is where the structural analysis in the earlier stages becomes really important. You have visualised the speech, figured out how it hooks together and used that visualisation to connect the paragraphs. Make sure you have some clue as to why each paragraph follows the one before. In almost every case, the next paragraph is either a) continuing this thought, or b) moving on to a related thought. In both cases, you can make it much easier by understanding why it flows like that. Convince yourself that this paragraph obviously has to follow that one, and you'll never forget the order.

Smoothing It Out

You're now at the point where you've got nearly all the sentences down, and most of the paragraphs, and you're able to get through the whole thing only looking at the book a few times. Now this is where you should not be reading quietly to yourself, but saying it aloud. When you're driving in the car, alone at home or whenever you have some privacy, try saying it all out loud, at full voice. Trust me, it sounds very different when you actually say it aloud. You'll find that you stumble more, and in different places. Some words turn out to be more difficult to pronounce than you expected. The earlier you start to say the words aloud, the less of an issue this becomes as you progress. Try it a few times. Start out by trying to do this frequently -- once, even twice every day. It'll be hard at first (and it's a real pain and extremely dangerous to pull out the ritual book while you're driving, SO DON'T! Record it onto a dictaphone or digital recorder), but it will gradually get easier.

When you're starting to feel comfortable, slow down, but don't stop. Practise it every couple of days, then every week. Don't slow down below once a week. If you feel up to it, see if you can speed up your recitation. This is only to be done during the memorisation process and never when you actually come to deliver the piece for real.

Chapter 6

Mindset

You are now at the point where you pretty much have the ritual memorised. Now, the trick is learning how to perform it well. Very nearly everyone has some amount of stage fright. Those of you who are acting types, the Thespian Freemason, often have it even worse than most. The trick to overcoming the nerves is to control the nerves.

What makes performing ritual or script for real different from the hours of practice in your car, or shower, or whilst walking your dog or in any other private place? Is it the people that will make you nervous? Is it maybe one particular person – someone you respect or admire, who you know can perform their ritual very well?

It may be something really stupid, like not being familiar with the surroundings, or you haven't performed it in regalia. You need to identify what it is that makes you nervous and remember that nerves are a positive, once you have them under some kind of control.

Have you ever heard the saying, "Face your fears to live your dreams"? Well, to do so you need to know your fears. Make a list of what your fears are.

Here is an idea of what makes me nervous when I'm performing ritual or speaking publicly.

- If I haven't put enough time into knowing what I'm doing.
- If I haven't visited the venue before.
- If the recipient is someone important to me. (I was invited to occupy the Worshipful Master's chair to initiate my nephew, Bro Jordan Hackett.)
- If I'm part of a team and have not worked with them before.

So what steps do I take to reduce the nerves to a level where I feel in control?

If I haven't been given time to prepare fully then I would consider asking for help from someone who has performed the ritual before, or organising a good prompt who would sit in close proximity to where I would be. It's important to make your prompter aware of how you want him to prompt. Make sure that whoever is going to prompt only does so you if you really need it. How many times has the confidence been destroyed by an overzealous prompter? You pause to move, or gather your thoughts, or maybe just for effect, and before you know it, the next line is hurled across the room at a speed and volume that breaks any concentration you had. I have, on occasion, asked the Lodge Director of Ceremonies (an office I held for a number of years, both at Lodge and Provincial level) to announce who the prompter was going to be and that no other prompting was necessary.

If I am not aware of my surroundings, then the first thing I would do is walk any perambulations I intend to make. This may sound silly but I can assure you that the last thing you need is to move to a spot in the only part of the room that has a squeaky floorboard or where the acoustics are just not viable. Anyone who knows me will be able to name the Masonic Hall I refer to . . . Yes, Halesowen Masonic Centre in Worcestershire, albeit a superb building, has the weirdest acoustics I have ever come across, and prior knowledge is a huge bonus. You may have performed this ritual in your own lodge room and feel really comfortable with it, but a different venue can easily throw you. Be aware!

In the case of my nephew Jordan, I have to admit that I put a little more effort into the preparation because I knew from experience that emotions would kick in and I would be focusing on him and making sure that he was OK. That was the responsibility of the Junior Deacon, not me, so I made sure that prior to the meeting I introduced my nephew to the Junior Deacon, who explained how the evening would go and to do exactly as directed and no more. By doing this I removed the need to be too concerned about my nephew, as he was in extremely capable hands.

Being part of a team doesn't mean that all will go well, even if you have put an enormous amount of effort into learning and preparing for your part. I always insist on a rehearsal or, at the very least, a get-together with the other participants, just so that we can all see how it fits together. Don't be afraid to insist on a rehearsal. The Lodge of Instruction Preceptor, another office I have held for a number of years, will appreciate your desire to "do a good job" and will always be willing to help.

You need to clarify what you want to get from a lodge rehearsal. In my opinion, you should be thinking of the whole team when at the rehearsal and not just the part that you will be playing in the forthcoming ceremony. Let's face it, if you have it all under control but one of the other officers doesn't, then that can, and more often than not will, have a negative impact on you and possibly on your performance.

Remember this . . .
Being nervous and being excited are so closely related. Don't be afraid of being nervous; be afraid of being unprepared.

That leads me into how to handle the situation when things go wrong.

For example, imagine that you have every base covered and the ritual and perambulations of the team are so well rehearsed that your confidence is high . . . then the unexpected happens . . . For example, the lodge is about to be opened in the Second Degree and you notice an Entered Apprentice is still present (obviously not the candidate for the evening). What do you do? Do you leap up and say, *"Worshipful Master . . . an imposter, an imposter."* Of course not. The Lodge Director of Ceremonies or his Assistant should have this in hand, but if it gets to the point where the ceremony is about to be compromised and no one has made a move to correct it, don't be shy; simply stand up and walk slowly towards the Lodge Director of Ceremonies and you will amazed how quiet it will go. Once you have made him aware, walk back to your seat and leave him to do his job. Never take on the role of another officer unless the Worshipful Master formally invites you so to do.

IMPORTANT: Never do this unless you are absolutely sure that you are correct. You will make yourself look silly and embarrass yourself. We don't want that to happen do we?

It's a difficult one, but I have seen it on a few occasions where the questions leading to the Second Degree have been asked and duly answered, the Deacon has taken the candidate to the Worshipful Master's pedestal and the secrets leading to the Second Degree have actually started to be explained and shared with the Candidate with an Entered Apprentice still present. I actually did exactly what I have suggested, as the lodge Director of Ceremonies had missed it. The simple fact that I stood up and made my way across the lodge room was enough to halt proceedings, thereby giving the Worshipful Master time to ask all below that of an Entered Apprentice, with the exception of the Candidate, to retire for a short while. I must be honest, that even with my experience I was a little nervous doing this, but no one else had noticed the potential screw up and it was a few seconds from being a double Second Degree ceremony. Oh yes . . . it wasn't my lodge.

Another tough one is when to interrupt if you feel that the ritual is going badly wrong. The simple answer is "Never!" The Lodge Director of Ceremonies has the sole responsibility for organising the relevant prompters for the evening and he and he only should be the backup. If the Immediate Past Master is failing to keep the ritual on track it will become evident. **You should never prompt unless you have been assigned that very responsibility – no matter how tempted you may be.**

How do you handle an overzealous prompter? That's something that must be sorted prior to the meeting. You must make sure that if you are performing ritual that may require a prompt that you talk to your prompter before the meeting and ensure that he is aware of what signal you will give him if you need one and that he delivers the prompt clearly. If he prompts you in a way other than the prearranged way, then don't be shy in asking him clearly to do as you have asked. I personally tell (not ask) anyone who may be required to prompt me, that he should only do so if I actually look at him. If you are pausing for effect and the overzealous prompter keeps chipping in, then you will be thrown completely and thereby your confidence will dissolve like a sugar lump in a hot cup of tea.

One of the most frustrating things that you will undoubtedly experience is an incorrect prompt. What do you do when you are given a prompt and are sure that it is wrong? Simple, you turn to your prompter and say quietly . . . *"Could you check that please?"* If he gives you the same prompt then the chances are that he is right and you are mistaken. If, however, you are absolutely sure that he is giving you the wrong prompt, ask to see the book and clarify it with him. At the end of the day, our ritual is a story and must flow. If you have missed a chunk out, for whatever reason, then the whole ceremony has a chance of becoming not only confused but also meaningless to the candidate.

Another situation that can and often does interrupt your mindset, is when you have physical things to consider, as well as remembering and delivering your words. The Lodge Deacon, for example, is not only responsible for the candidate, but also has a Deacon's wand to juggle. I remember when I became the lodge Junior Deacon, my brother Senior Deacon and I worked so hard to make the wand a part of our physical being that we didn't have to think *"What do I do with my wand whilst I'm giving a particular salute, or moving the candidate from one part of the lodge room to another?"*

Acting

Now that you're comfortable with your mindset, observe how you do it. By now, you're not thinking about it so much; your mouth is doing almost all the work, with the conscious mind simply making a few connections between paragraphs and then physical requirements that so often accompany Masonic ritual.

That is the right state to be in. Think about how that feels. Before you go in to "perform" do some basic acting exercises. Take a few deep breaths and concentrate on not thinking. I think the ideal is a little light meditation, but it takes a fair bit of practice to be able to drop into that state on demand. For now, just focus on being calm.

Being calm is far more important than anything else. If you're calm, you're unlikely to screw up too badly. If you're tense, you're far more likely to. Some people like to exercise the body a bit, and relax the mind. You should do what works for you.

There will be occasions when you just can't get the words exactly as the book – don't panic! Some of the best delivered ritual is not verbatim. In fact, I can think of one very experienced Freemason, who just happens to be one of my sponsors into Freemasonry, W.Bro Colin Young, PSGD, Assistant PGM of Worcestershire, who can pull ceremonies of many and varied degrees, right out of thin air . . . or at least it appears that way. Colin has, on many occasions, been asked at the eleventh hour to perform a piece of ritual. I remember one occasion when he was asked to present the Royal Arch Mystical Lecture, literally as we were walking into the temple. It had been eight years since he had last delivered this lecture, but typical Colin, he sat with the ritual book, whilst performing his duties as Scribe E, and when the time came, delivered the most interesting and informative Mystical Lecture I have ever heard. The words were all there but the prompter had no chance whatsoever in being able to prompt. In fact, he actually closed the ritual book, sat back and enjoyed the lecture.

OK, not everyone can do this and it does require experience, but it simply demonstrates the need to understand the story so well that thinking of the exact words becomes less of a challenge.

Chapter 7

Recognising Learning Barriers

Remember; if you tell yourself often enough that you can't do something, you will probably be correct! – Positive mental attitude is one of the keys to doing one's best.

"The trick is not to underestimate someone's ability, because of the foreseen disability."

Interestingly, when we work with people who do have a disability, such as a sight issue, the sighted person who is helping often becomes the student. Never assume that someone is incapable of doing something just because they are blind, deaf or have other physical disabilities. Ask them if they need help and if they say "No" then trust that they are capable. I feel sure that you will agree that those of us who are not so physically challenged should always be ready to help others but must never force our good intentions on them!

Visual Impairment

There are many members of Freemasonry who have, in varying degrees, some form of visual impairment. It's difficult to give absolute guidance on how those with this barrier should approach learning their ritual, as someone with total blindness will have more physical challenges with regard to learning, and in particular delivering ritual, than someone with partial blindness. The latter can at least partially see those taking part and the physical layout of the lodge room, whereas someone totally blind will have many more challenges. Interestingly, someone who was born blind copes better than someone whose loss of sight is a relatively recent event.

Up until recently, there was a Braille version of the Emulation ritual which was no doubt very costly to produce and rarely sold – hence it is currently no longer available. With technology moving at a rate difficult to keep up with, there are many methods of recording voice and text onto computers. The Voice Recognition Software available now in comparison with say five years ago is much less expensive and far more accurate. For a sighted person to assist a visually impaired person in this way is a most useful and relatively easy thing to do.

A report by the World Health Organization states that there are four levels of visual function:

- normal vision
- moderate visual impairment
- severe visual impairment
- blindness

Each of these levels will present different challenges to the brother who is keen to take part in the ceremonies and indeed to progress through the various offices. If we do one thing in their early Masonic development, it should be to make them aware that we are there to help in whatever way we can – exactly as we should with any new brother. I suppose, given the different levels of need and varying drive and determination of the individual, we should simply establish, by asking, the level of assistance required.

You may ask questions such as:

"Is there a need to hoodwink a candidate for initiation if he is blind?"

or,

"How do we handle the part of the ritual that gives the candidate light?"

One must remember that much of what we do and say is symbolic, and the hoodwink is used, in part, for that very reason. As for the candidate being given light, I truly believe that the spiritual light we give a new initiate is far more valuable than physical light!

Remember, that if an individual's senses are challenged, then the brain, in conjunction with the determination of the individual, calls on the remaining senses to compensate.

Hearing Impairment

For some deaf and hard of hearing Freemasons, background noise can be heard but human speech is difficult to understand. Many buildings are fitted with an induction loop which when linked to a hearing aid amplifies words. The hearing loop picks up the sounds which are spoken into a microphone and can make them more distinct, but other background conversations and noises, not picked up by the system, are not heard.

People who become deaf after they've learned to speak may be able to speak sufficiently well and give a misleading impression that they can hear quite well. This is when we need to ask if a known hearing-impaired brother requires any assistance. It may be something as simple as making sure that his prompter (if he's delivering a piece of ritual) is placed in a position that is close enough for the brother to hear, or lip-read. So often we see, for example, the Immediate Past Master prompting from such a long way off that he sometimes has to shout to make himself heard. There is absolutely nothing wrong with asking for your prompter to be sat close by. Another useful suggestion, if one is perambulating and delivering ritual, is to have more than one prompt.

When it comes to learning techniques, someone with a hearing impairment of a more severe degree is more likely to rely on his visual senses. This can present challenges, as to see what is happening and to read what is happening can be dreadfully hampered if at the same time they need to take on board what someone is saying, either by lip-reading or sign language. When you consider that a significant amount of Masonic ritual is performed with dimmed lighting, you can see the potential issues with regard to prompting.

I guess the tip here is to ask the brother concerned what he would suggest, as after all, he's more qualified to tell us how we can help – it's simply a case of making sure we ask!

Dyslexia and Dysgraphia

Interestingly, many people who we categorise as lazy may suffer from a learning difficulty. Now that's not to say that they have a below average level of intelligence; to the contrary, in many cases people with learning difficulties, such as dyslexia or dysgraphia, are highly intelligent and have very successful careers. They are often very hard-working individuals who have had to prove themselves because of their learning issues.

How many people know what dyslexia or dysgraphia actually are?

People who have dyslexia may have a difficulty with the use of both written and oral language. This is due in part to processing difficulties, including visual and auditory perceptual skills, and is not necessarily related to their academic history. They sometimes find that certain learning tasks are a cause concern. This can be due to difficulties with short-term memory, concentration and organisation.

It's important for people to recognise that dyslexia is not an intellectual disability, since dyslexia and IQ are not interrelated.

What is dyslexia?

The word "dyslexic" is based on two Greek words: "dys" meaning "difficulty" and "lexic" meaning "with words". Dyslexia is a condition that you are born with, a difference in the way the brain works, a difference that will be present throughout your life. Dyslexia mainly affects reading and language skills and can range from mild to very severe. The sooner dyslexia is spotted, the sooner suitable learning and coping strategies can be employed to minimise the effects of the condition.

Some of the indicating factors of dyslexia are:

Phonological processing. This is the breaking down of words into their component sounds and at the same time trying to comprehend their meaning. If you read a word that you find difficult in the first instance to see, then the understanding of that word will more than likely be difficult.

Poor spelling. Often dyslexics have difficulty in structuring certain words and thereby the transfer of a word from the brain to the page presents spelling issues.

Hesitant reading. This is the factor that most identifies dyslexics. Whilst often very articulate in conversation, the person affected has difficulty in transporting the written word from the eye, via the brain, and into the spoken word.

What is dysgraphia?

Dysgraphia is a difficulty in writing, where written work may be illegible and inaccurately spelled. This difficulty may exist in varying degrees and does not match with either the person's intelligence, which may be above average, or their ability to read. There is often a lack of co-ordination and fine motor skills. I know how frustrating this is as I have been a sufferer for many years. Interestingly, Freemasonry and the study of how best to perform my ritual have helped tremendously. My written work is much clearer and my spelling, albeit still frustrating, has improved significantly. I know many people who initially thought that they were dyslexic but were in fact just like me!

So, having identified the fundamental challenges, how can we help?

I would suggest that any brother who is dyslexic should be made aware of the help available. I know from experience that it would be wrong and indeed un-Masonic to expect the brother to be able to pick up a ritual book and learn in the conventional manner (if there is a conventional manner). It has been proved that, as mentioned before, when one sense struggles, the other senses compensate. So to read words at the same time as listening to them aids the phonological processing as well as adding a recognised sound to a word, or words, that from the page are not as clear as one would wish. If you were to electronically record the ritual then ask the brother to first listen to the recording and then subsequently listen **and** read, the difficulty one has with the structure of words is eased by the assistance of the recorded sound.

I also believe that if you understand the ritual completely, this will reduce the composite pressure of, a) comprehension, b) alliteration and c) pronunciation.

There is, of course, the basic lack of ability to read and write. Not that this is common amongst Freemasons, but there are those who just can't read or write, or have limited ability. Does that make them less of a Freemason? No, of course not, but it does present additional challenges that many of us do not have to cope with. Having been to a lodge and witnessed this, I was most impressed at the obvious and extreme effort that one particular brother had committed to. The result of months of effort was almost word-perfect ritual. If there was a medal for effort then this brother deserved it. I suppose it showed me, and others, that he had found his learning method and worked strenuously to do the best he could.

It would be wrong for me to give the impression that I am academically qualified to offer a definitive interpretation of the difficulties people have with regard to the barriers I have mentioned, or to say that this is the correct and only way to help, but from personal experiences I know that with the honesty of the individual and the readiness to help of others, there is always a way forward.

The saddest thing I witness is when a "supposed mentor" doesn't recognise the needs of others and takes on the role of a mentor only for their own selfish reasons . . . "Look at me. I know more than you!" So often an obvious case of kudos!

Did you know that if you tell someone often enough that they can't do something, they will eventually believe you. What's even worse is when you frequently tell yourself that you can't do something and eventually prove yourself right.

Stop that right now and believe in yourself . . . others will follow.

Chapter 8

Acting

Now for the final nuance. This separates merely competent ritual from the really good stuff. Now that you're able to let your mouth do all the talking, start listening to yourself. Think about the ritual again, but don't think about the words, think about what it means:

- What are the important bits? Emphasise those
- How could you use your body or hands to illustrate a point?
- Try talking to the person in front of you, not just at them. Look them in the eye and make them get the point.
- You are teaching important lessons here; try to capture a little of the emotional intensity of that importance.

Talking about stumbling, it's quite possible that you will have put all the hard work into the learning process, gearing yourself up for a cracking performance, got your mindset just right and something distracts you in mid-flow! How do you handle that? If you are not careful, or indeed have failed to have this eventuality covered, your confidence can very quickly be destroyed. There are many suggestions that I can offer, but they would be based on personal experience and like many aspects of understanding, learning and delivering ritual, we cope with the composite structure in different ways.

So let me give you a few simple yet critical pointers:

Firstly, be prepared to stop and start at unexpected periods during the delivery. If you find that the distraction is due to another brother losing his flow and subsequently throwing you into confusion, make absolutely sure that you focus on **your words** and perambulations and **not his!** If you have understood the ritual totally and made yourself aware of the other parts of the ritual, then you may be in the strong position of helping him out; maybe whisper his line to him, for example. Be careful that you don't leap in and throw him off; he may be pausing for effect or some other valid reason. The key is to work as a team. That is why the **team** rehearsal is crucial.

Another useful tip is to make sure that the elected prompter (you will remember how strongly I emphasised the need to establish that prior to the meeting) is aware that he only prompts when he sees the perspiration dripping from your nose, or some other prearranged signal. I always tell the prompter that if I go quiet for what seems to be an unusual period of time and give him the look of desperation, then he can prompt, but not before!

It's also very important that he gives you a prompt that you can hear. For some reason, some people who prompt feel that they should whisper the lead word or words, probably to hide the fact that you need help. Equally frustrating is the prompter who feels the need to bellow it across the room, just to show others that he is needed and on the ball. However, if he prompts me too quickly, the look he will see is one of . . . *"You wait 'till I see you after the meeting . . ."* Of course I'm only kidding. I would be tactful and very diplomatic in my post-meeting chat with him about prompting techniques. *(This is where I would add a smiley face if I were texting or emailing this paragraph.)*

"Take a prompt, it's not a crime"
Seriously, though, get all this sorted well in advance and leave nothing to chance.

What not to do when the moment of terror strikes and you go completely blank:

Never apologise . . . *"Sorry Worshipful Master, may I start that again?"* What's he going to say? *"NO."* Of course not! Just start again and you will be surprised how often your glitch will go unnoticed.

Having spent six years on the Provincial circuit, latterly as Provincial Deputy Grand Director of Ceremonies, I have witnessed many people make mistakes or die on the masonic stage and the most frustrating thing I have ever seen is the brother who makes a mistake (and don't forget that the man who doesn't make a mistake is doing nothing), subsequently walks around the room visibly reprimanding himself... Why? It's too late, so don't worry... move on.

Back to the Acting

It's not a bad idea to think of your Masonic clothing and regalia as costume. Ensure that your clothing and regalia look the part. If you look scruffy then you will be perceived as scruffy, even if your ritual is acceptable. If you feel good about yourself, then others will buy into your performance even before you start.

Just imagine, you could well be one of the first masonically clad Freemasons a candidate may see. What impression will he have of our wonderful Craft if he sees an untidy individual, with his apron hanging under his stomach, a dirty shirt collar and scuffed and dirty shoes? OK, I hear you say, *"Why is he banging on about appearance when all I want to do is find out how to learn ritual?"* The answer is simple . . . it matters and is a crucial part of the whole process. If you look good then you will feel good!

As mentioned in detail in the earlier chapter which covers Maslow's hierarchy, the synchronisation of one's physiological and psychological needs is truly important. I think you may now see how the melding of your physical being and your psyche can play an important part in getting it right on the night.

Your voice should simply be considered as a tool of your trade. Even if you have all other bases covered, all can go terribly wrong if your delivery is too quick or too quiet. Spend time practising your delivery. When you feel you have the pace right, slow it down even more. Your adrenalin will naturally speed up your delivery, so you need to be aware. Also your volume is important. If you speak too quietly then other brethren taking part may not be clear when they have to come in.

A trick I use when practising my ritual aloud is to speak in a theatrical-type voice. I use a Noel Coward voice which always brings a smile to my wife's face if she happens to hear me practising . . . sounds silly, but it works for me.

Staying Open is an acting term which refers to the position of your body relative to your audience. If you are speaking to someone, then make sure that you are facing them. Imagine that you are in conversation with an individual – you wouldn't have your back to them, would you? Apart from the fact that it would appear rude, it would also be difficult to make your point. Have the courtesy of looking someone in the eye; that way you will almost definitely demonstrate conviction in the message that you are attempting to deliver.

When you are delivering ritual that requires props, such as Working Tools, make sure that you use them correctly. Be familiar with them and have the confidence to demonstrate them rather than just explain them. This is something that you should do right from the start.

How to use your body when delivering ritual

Just imagine that you are in handcuffs when you are next having a conversation with someone. Try not to move your hands or involve your body in the conversation. How unnatural does that feel? You would never talk to anyone with just your voice. Your hands and indeed your whole body are how you reinforce the words you use. If you are being direct with someone, you would maybe point at them (rude, I know, but we all do it from time to time). Gesticulating is natural. You don't have to think about it in day-to-day conversation, so don't do it with your ritual. The more natural you can make your delivery, the clearer and more convincing the message becomes.

An absolute "No-No" is invading a person's space. Ensure that you don't stand so close (unless the ritual calls for it) that the recipient is focusing on the fact that you are too close and not on the message that you are attempting to relay.

Be careful not to overact

If you try too hard it can come across as overacting. Think of your words as conversational. Don't think about it too much. How would you say it in normal day-to-day conversation? Would you over-exaggerate it? Of course you wouldn't. Just be yourself.

There are many examples of how this can make a real difference in Masonic ritual. One that springs to mind is a line in the Holy Royal Arch exaltation ceremony . . . *"We would scorn to be descended from those who basely fled . . ."* This is a statement of defence and needs emphasis on the word "scorn".

This is where knowing each other's lines is important. You can react naturally much better if you are not surprised by what the other person is saying.

Finally, a very useful idea is to practise in front of a mirror, preferably a full-length mirror. That way you can see what others will see, and if you don't like what you see, how can you expect others to?

Chapter 9

The Mentoring Scheme

Many of you will have heard of the Mentoring Scheme which started to be encouraged in the Provinces by The United Grand Lodge of England in 2008. So what is the Mentoring Scheme? Why did Grand Lodge go to so much trouble to investigate the validity of such a scheme, a scheme that Industry and Commerce have favoured for many years, and, of course, how can it help you with the learning process?

Ask yourself the question. If you have personally taken the time and effort to become a good ritualist and thereby a better Mason, would you expect to be simply left alone to get on with it? The answer is "No". The Mentoring Scheme will undoubtedly enhance your efforts and give you the ongoing access to, and the support of, the more experienced Mason that you so deserve. This is not a baby-sitting exercise but a "must have" regular update on where you are and where you are going in your Masonic career. You wouldn't be expected to work alone in any academic or commercial position without some form of mentoring, would you? So why not take advantage of this wonderful initiative? Take my advice and insist that your lodge grabs the Mentoring Scheme with both hands and watch the quality of work within your lodge improve. The first thing your lodge will need to do is carefully choose an experienced Past Master to co-ordinate and manage it. He won't be expected to be the Lodge mentor to all junior brethren (those below the Worshipful Master's chair), but should be able to allocate the work to a number of equally experienced brethren who are willing to take the responsibility seriously.

Here is the **Ritual section from the Mentoring Tool Kit** used in my own Province of Worcestershire, which has been compiled and edited by my dear friend W.Bro Nick Cripps, the Provincial Grand Mentor, who has been instrumental over the past few years bringing about Mentoring not only in in this Province but also nationally.

Ritual

"Historically, by not reading the Ritual, all were enabled to take part, even those of low standards of literacy. Additionally, not committing the Ritual to print emphasised its secrecy which was fashionable at that time. Neither can it be denied that the ceremony has far more impact on the Candidate when delivered from memory.

Freemasonry endeavours to teach moral lessons and self-knowledge to new members. However, it is one thing to have aims and ideals and quite another to impress them upon the minds of the members. So, in our Lodge rooms we enact, for the benefit of the new member, what can be likened to the scenes from a play. The scenes are called degrees, because Freemasonry is a progressive system. The play is centred on the building of King Solomon's Temple where **every part of the building and every implement used is given a deeper moral or spiritual interpretation,** which is explained to the new member.

In many Lodges, a Candidate does not have access to the printed ritual until he is presented with, or allowed to purchase, a ritual book following the completion of his Third Degree. It is highly unlikely that the candidate will then have either the time or the energy to study all three ceremonies, so he should be provided with a copy of the ritual immediately after each ceremony, that he may read it and raise any questions while the events are reasonably fresh in his mind.

He should be made aware that there are many versions of Masonic ritual, with differences not only apparent at a national level owing to language, but also regionally and even between Lodges meeting in close proximity to each other. Very different ceremonials have evolved often with distinct signs, movements and customs (and regalia is also extremely varied throughout the world, from plain and simple to highly colourful and elaborate). All Masonic ritual, however, has the same purpose – to make Masons and to educate them further in the tenets of the Craft and their derivation.

Originally, each Lodge in England seems to have had its own ritual, more or less following a common pattern but, since many relied on memory rather than the precise written word, differing in content. After the union of the two Grand Lodges – the Ancients and the Moderns – in 1813, the Lodge of Reconciliation (which had been formed to bring the union about) continued its work by agreeing one set of ceremonies for acceptance by the united body. It was approved by Grand Lodge in 1816 and is, essentially, the ritual still in regular usage today, further refined by the Emulation Lodge of Improvement founded in 1823. Though very many private Lodges may have their own idiosyncrasies, of word or movement here and there, it is primarily the Emulation working that is in common use throughout the English Constitution.

Impress upon the Candidate that the Ritual is a book to be studied, since it carefully provides not only the words and an idea of the movements to be used in the ceremonies, but also an insight into the thinking and intentions that inspired Freemasonry. This is part of the reason why each participating Mason is required to learn his words rather than simply reading them – by the repetition and concentration that the learning entails, understanding and appreciation grows. And with greater familiarity comes recognition, acceptance and enjoyment so the process of learning is an essential part of the Freemason's education into the Craft and, hopefully, his subsequent lifestyle. An integral part of the 'beneficial effect'.

Thus, it is important that time and effort be assiduously given when learning is to be done, so that the ceremony can be given as flawlessly as possible. For this reason too, attendance at rehearsals is essential. A well conducted ceremony not only impresses the candidate, but also demonstrates to him his importance, shown by the fact that so many of his new-found Brethren have gone to such lengths for his benefit and to ensure his welcome amongst them. It does of course also provide them with huge satisfaction in a job well done with skill and co-operation.

However long or short the piece of ritual, you should always endeavour to deliver it with clarity and sincerity. If mumbled or garbled, the message will be lost and with it the purpose, not to mention the recipient's attention and interest. Having said that, it is acknowledged that very few of us are professional actors, so **all that is expected is that members try their hardest, do their very best and accept the guidance of the Director of Ceremonies."**

Back in 2008 the powers that be established the need to ensure, if the process is followed, that our new and junior members were taken care of. It had become evident that for many years Freemasonry had become guilty of simply getting members and not getting good Masons. Very

Worshipful Jeffrey Gillyon, Past Grand Sword Bearer, summed up how to handle the issue by using what he referred to as "an old saying", *"Putting Masonry into Men – not just Men into Masonry"*.

This very wise brother goes on to say, *". . . we all know Masons who never bother to learn any ritual. Perhaps even more disturbing, I suspect we all know many more that are very good at ritual, but never give a thought to its meaning and how it translates into our everyday lives."*

The learning process starts the day that you decide to become a Freemason. *"Why?"* I hear you ask . . . *"I don't have to learn any ritual for my home visit or interview with the Past Masters, do I?"* Of course not, but, as you will find out from reading this book, learning ritual is not simply learning the words. A good understanding of what Freemasonry **was about, is about** and **can be about** is so very important. In other words, a study of the history of Freemasonry and where the various orders originated from and how they all fit together (A great book by Keith Jackson called *Beyond the Craft* is well worth a read.)

Is about because it gives you a good idea of what Freemasonry is today and the reasons why we do what we do, and when I say **can be about** I say this simply because Freemasonry can mean so many things to different people. The deeper you look, the more options you will find and the more that Freemasonry will impact on your day-to-day life.

Freemasonry has so much more for you to discover, if only you have the desire and know-how to look.

So who is involved and how does the Mentoring Scheme work?

The Mentor

A mentor, if you look it up in the Oxford Dictionary, is "an inexperienced person's advisor". Even though the sponsors of a candidate are often seen as the obvious choice, this, in many cases, does not work; it may be that the proposer or seconder holds an office in lodge and is not able to sit with the mentee. It may be that he too is inexperienced. I remember when I had only been a Freemason for one year; I saw the benefits that would suit a dear friend of mine and talked the Past Masters of my lodge into allowing me to be his proposer. I certainly wasn't experienced enough to be his mentor!

A brother's personal mentor fits nicely into the Mentoring Scheme provided that he follows the tried and tested programme produced with the encouragement of United Grand Lodge. It is a mentor's responsibility to ensure that the new Mason is made to feel welcome, progressively understands Freemasonry and is aware of what is required of him as a new Freemason. A mentor really needs to be enthusiastic, approachable, a good communicator and a knowledgeable Freemason.

The Candidate

It is the new member's responsibility to simply buy into the programme and commit via his involvement in the lodge activities. Of course there will be work to do; this is inevitable when one wishes to expand knowledge and progress. Fear not, though; a mentor will provide guidelines on how best to achieve the various goals.

Most importantly, the whole process should – no, must – be enjoyable. I'm sure that you will agree that if we enjoy what we do, we do it better!

The Lodge

Ideally, each Lodge has a responsibility to look after its members and to ensure that a mentor is appointed for each new candidate (or existing candidate if not already appointed). Lodges may adopt various procedures for doing this, but ideally the Worshipful Master is best placed to appoint to the newly created office of mentor a senior and experienced brother to fulfil the role co-ordinating the lodge mentors. It would not be practical or indeed very successful for the mentor to shoulder the responsibility of acting as a personal mentor for, as we have seen, every candidate will have different needs and varying levels of dependency. It's also important to pair brethren so that they have a mutual level of respect and therefore the line of communication is easier to travel.

The general format goes like this:

Right at the very beginning, from the time that a prospective candidate makes contact with the lodge, the mentoring programme should commence. That is to say that he should instantly be made to feel welcome and be offered answers to his many questions, and where necessary, answers to questions that he has not even thought of, such as the financial and personal commitment. To ensure that the scheme is followed correctly, there are always four key elements:

- Identify the needs of the mentee.
- Identify the source of the information required.
- Identify who is responsible for looking after the mentee: the lodge mentor, the proposer, or other experience brother.
- The timescale required (must be achievable and agreed).

The structure of the Mentoring Scheme is there primarily to protect the new and junior Freemason from failing to cement his relationship with his fellow brethren and the Craft. This is a sad situation that has been evidenced due to the lack of some form of mentoring resulting in a number of junior brethren going through their First, Second and maybe Third Degree ceremonies and then falling by the wayside, either by resigning or simply repeatedly not attending their lodge meetings.

An anonymous Freemason wrote the following:

I'm the Guy[1]

"I'm the guy sitting by himself on the side. I asked to join, I paid my dues and I promised to be faithful and loyal. I've come to the meetings, but hardly anyone pays attention to me. I've tried to be part of the group but everyone seems to talk to and sit with their own friends. I want to get involved, but I'm not sure how to do it. The same guys always seem to do the work but they don't seem interested in having anyone new join them. I missed a few meetings after joining, and no one asked me at the next meeting where I had been. Everyone says 'Hi,' but no one really seems interested in me. I want to get involved, I want to know more. I want to be part of the group, but right now I'm thinking about the game I'm missing on TV.

Are you that guy or do you know a brother who is that guy? If so then talk to someone about how the Mentoring Scheme can or should be implemented in your lodge!

---

1   *Author unknown, but thank you anyway*

About the Author

Andrew Skidmore, married to Cheryl, co-author of *A Handbook for The Freemason's Wife* has three sons and lives in Worcestershire. He was initiated into the Lodge of Hope and Charity No 377 in January 1992. Andrew has been a Lodge of Instruction Preceptor for a number of years and is a member of the Worcestershire Provincial Training and Education team. As the founding Director of Ceremonies of the George Taylor Research Lodge No. 9819, the ritual and research elements of Freemasonry are dear to his heart.

His first appointment in the Craft was that of Provincial Grand Steward, progressing on to Provincial Deputy Grand Director of Ceremonies. Andrew has been appointed to acting rank in the Holy Royal Arch and the Mark Degree. He is also 30° in the Ancient and Accepted Rite and active in many other orders.